# Sea Friends and Selfies

## Ocean Conservation for Children

by **Erin Edwards**

This book is dedicated
to my ocean-loving
Dad, Steve Edwards,
"Stevie," the orca.

Sea Friends and Selfies

Ocean Conservation for Children

Erin Edwards

ISBN: 978-1-66789-818-6

There was once an olive ridley sea turtle named Willa. She was born on a beautiful empty beach in Mexico with mangroves that met the soft, golden sand and a sparkling blue sea. Now that she was grown, it was time for her to lay her eggs and wait for baby sea turtles to hatch on that same beach. This was a special beach. It was the same beach that Willa was born, Willa's mother was born, Willa's grandmother was born and so on.

However, looking around, Willa noticed a change to this beach. She saw plastic bottles and bottle caps, plastic straws, potato chip bags, deflated balloons and other trash.

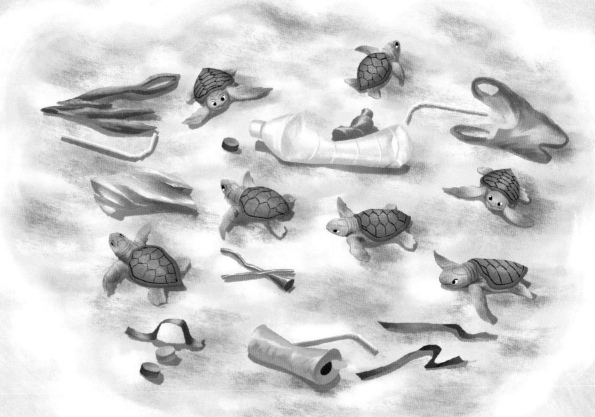

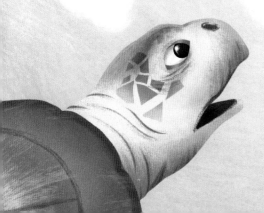

She fussed and fretted all night that her hatchlings might eat these items and get very, very sick.

Willa decided to hold an emergency meeting with her ocean friends. She called Colton, the octopus; Deacon, the gray whale; Nolan, the humpback whale; Audrey, the spinner dolphin; Stevie, the orca; Charlie, the elephant seal; Taryn, the blue marlin; Davie, the leatherback turtle; Hannah, the amberjack; Nickie, the black tip shark; and Sammy, the scalloped hammerhead shark.

All her ocean friends agreed
that something must be done.

"I swallowed three bottle caps by mistake just yesterday!" Audrey said.

"I thought a plastic bag was a jelly fish and I swallowed it whole!" Nolan yelled.

"I know! I had a helium balloon with fish for lunch. Yuck!" Charlie cried.

Stevie, the orca, known for creative solutions, said, "I have an idea. Humans love to take selfies or photos with us when they spot us. What if we put their trash in the photo so they HAVE to see the problem."

So the next day, when Deacon, the gray whale, showed his whale tail to a group of people on a boat, he first made sure to wrap his tail with balloons.

When Davie, the leatherback sea turtle, came into the shallow water and a woman on the beach took a selfie with him, he made sure to have bright plastic straws coming out of his mouth.

When Audrey, the spinner dolphin, twirled and jumped and swam along side a boat of tourists going out to sea, she made sure to have a plastic bottle hanging out of her mouth.

Colton, the octopus, got really excited because he has eight arms so he could really show these humans the problem.

He knew they even take pictures of themselves underwater so this idea could really work. He wrapped one arm in a green potato chip bag, another arm in a plastic bag, another arm in a soda bottle and another arm in decorative ribbons. He swam by a group of snorkelers and, sure enough, snap, snap, snap. Success!

Later that night, the humans got ready to upload, tag, post and caption their photos, but then they stopped and exclaimed,

"What is this in the photo?"

One little girl shouted, "We must do something about the trash in our oceans!" The next day the humans held an urgent meeting. As every little bit counts towards protecting the oceans, they decided to do the following:

- Use reusable water bottles to refill their water instead of using plastic bottles.
  - Bring their own bags when grocery shopping.
  - Never use plastic straws or utensils.
  - Pick up their trash.
  - Limit their single-use items.
  - Recycle everything.

The news about the meeting spread to the sea animals and they sighed with relief. "This calls for a celebration!" Stevie exclaimed. There was more work to be done, but this was an excellent start. They had a big party that night.

**Erin Edwards** is completing her Master's Degree in Environmental Studies and Sustainability from Unity College and has a Bachelor's Degree in Writing and Literature from California State University at San Marcos. She has been a Corporate Flight Attendant, traveling the world, since 2015. In her late teens and twenties, Erin competed and traveled for surfing. It was this time in the ocean that Erin developed a passion for the ocean and desire to protect it. Erin also writes articles and produces video interviews for The Inertia and others, focusing on people and companies that have new ideas on how to protect the environment. Erin started a company to connect people with similar passions, Sea 2 Snow, a few years ago. She resides in Oceanside, California.